Dog
in the
Manger

Tim Schenck

Illustrations by Jay Sidebotham
Book design by Amy Goldberg Svihlik

ISBN 978-0-88028-371-7

Printed in USA

Forward Movement
www.forwardmovement.org

Dedication

To my mother, Lois,
whose lessons on language
included the wonderful phrase
"Dog in the Manger."
I'm grateful that her gift,
as well as her passion,
for writing was
more-or-less hereditary.

Acknowledgments

It never fails to amaze me that my family has yet to evict me. Of course that would be awkward since we live in a church rectory, and I'm the rector. In my wife Bryna, I'm blessed with a beautiful and talented woman who ensures I do things other than work, drink coffee, and write. My boys Benedict and Zachary continue to be a source of pride as they discover their own interests and passions.

Since they're featured in some of these essays, please don't tell them this book exists.

I love being a parish priest, and I'm privileged to exercise this ministry at a special place on Boston's South Shore: The Episcopal Parish of St. John the Evangelist in Hingham, Massachusetts. If you're ever in the neighborhood, stop by!

I'm grateful to the talented Richelle Thompson for shepherding this project to completion and to the entire Forward Movement staff for making it happen.

A word of gratitude to social media maven Meredith Gould for commenting on a number of these essays in draft form.

I was thrilled when priest and cartoonist Jay Sidebotham agreed to illustrate this book, and I'm well aware that many of you bought it because you thought it was one of his famous cartoon calendars.

And finally, as much as it pains me, I must thank my online "archnemesis," Lent Madness co-conspirator, and Forward Movement Executive Director, the Rev. Scott Gunn. This Church of ours is a lot more fun and vibrant with you in it—though if anyone asks me, I'll deny having ever said this.

Table of Contents

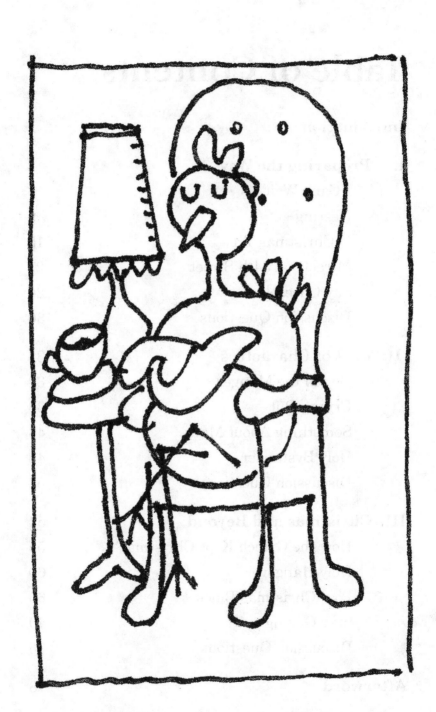

Introduction

When I was a kid, we received a Christmas card from friends who lived on a farm with their five children. On the outside was a photograph of the family arranged in a traditional pose—everyone dressed in their Sunday best, sitting nicely at a picnic table outside the barn and smiling for the camera. Even the family chicken was peacefully posed, front and center on the lap of one of the kids. But when you opened up the card, there was another shot of the family. This one showed everyone laughing and whooping it up with chicken feathers flying all over the place.

Around the holidays, many of us try to keep up the Norman Rockwell image of perfection while living with the chaotic reality that runs beneath it all. Finding faith amid frenzy is the true spiritual challenge of the season. One path would be to enter a monastery for the month of December, though good luck telling your spouse, kids, family, and friends about this plan. They may have you committed some place with padded walls rather than stone ones. The other option is to find God in the very midst of your Christmas chaos—and that is what this little book seeks to demonstrate.

As a clergy family, my wife and I try to keep the magic of the holidays alive for our children and for ourselves. Like any family, sometimes we succeed, and sometimes we fall short. Being a "professional" Christian doesn't change the often-elusive attempt to live faithfully and impart spiritual values to our children while juggling the demands of our fast-paced, hyper-connected lives. Holidays just add to the degree of difficulty.

A good metaphor for faith around the holidays may be found in the way I wrap Christmas presents. Unlike my wife Bryna, who wraps gifts as if she works in a Hallmark store (which she did while in high school), I'm the worst wrapper this side of the North Pole. It's embarrassing: tape and paper everywhere, ends and corners sticking out, and a ribbon two sizes too big. There's a gift in there somewhere—it just takes a while to find. This past Christmas, I gave up and wrapped Bryna's present in plastic grocery store bags. Little did the cashier know when she asked if

I preferred "paper or plastic" that she was serving as my own personal elf.

Our faith is a gift, but it isn't a perfectly wrapped present with exact folds and a precisely tied bow. It's more like the way I wrap. Fortunately faith isn't about being neat and tidy. You may burn the Christmas roast, Santa may not bring your child exactly what she wanted, you might even get sick and miss out on the best party of the year. But through it all, God remains.

On the surface, there are precious few moments of prayerful silence in these reflections. But if you dig a bit deeper, you'll see God's presence in each encounter. At the end of each chapter, I've provided some questions to use for personal reflection or group study. I hope the experiences shared here will resonate and mirror your own family's ever-evolving efforts to make it through Christmas with your sanity intact and your faith engaged.

– Tim Schenck

Dog
in the
Manger

I. PREPARING THE WAY

I Can't Wait!

"I can't wait!"

We have, shall we say, patience issues at our house. They go well beyond the fact that I can't wait until baseball season starts. (How many days until pitchers and catchers report for spring training?) Most kids are hard-wired for instant gratification. They want what they want, and they want it now. If patience is a virtue, we're not living very virtuously. Whenever commercials come on in between episodes of SpongeBob or Power Rangers, I hear a steady stream of "I want that toy," "I want to see that movie," and "I want to go to McDonald's." Despite the slogan, I'm not "lovin' it." Scripture says one day is like "a thousand years" in God's sight (Psalm 90:4). For young children, the ten minutes it takes to get home from the barber is like an eternity in their sight. This lack of patience seems particularly acute around birthdays and certain holidays—usually the ones involving presents or candy. They can wait the

138 days until Groundhog Day. It's the twenty-eight days until Christmas that gives them fits.

To be fair, the waiting is pretty hard for birthdays too. Soon after Christmas, my son Zack enters countdown mode for his birthday on February 15. He gets so focused on that date, I feel like I should create an Advent-like calendar just for Zack to properly observe the season of "Zackvent." In preparation for his seventh birthday, Zack designed his own cake. He handed Bryna a drawing of an ornate cake with seven layers, to mark each year with a different colored frosting, of course. Then he announced, "Have the bakery make this. Oh, and since it's a Godzilla party, top it with a fire-breathing monster."

I can just imagine the blank look from the teenager behind the counter. "Can I interest you in a Fudgie the Whale cake?" Uh, no. Unless you can make flames fly out of Fudgie's mouth with a can of Sterno.

Advent, the season of waiting for the coming of the Christ Child, is difficult for all of us. It's particularly hard for Christians who take their faith seriously because waiting is such a counter-cultural discipline. We dread waiting rooms so much we stock them with blaring televisions and bad coffee to dull our pain. In our society where the norm is if-you-have-an-itch-scratch-it, intentional waiting is suspect.

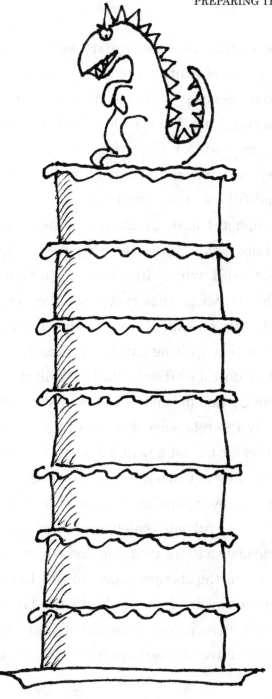

As Christians, we actively mark and celebrate this Advent season of waiting not because we're into self-denial, but because waiting is an important feature of the spiritual life. We wait for God's answers when we pray; we wait for Christ's self-revelation during daily life; and we wait for those glimpses of heaven on earth that fill our lives with hope.

The prophet Isaiah proclaims, "Those who wait for the Lord shall renew their strength, they shall mount up with wings like eagles" (Isaiah 40:31). While this is where that overly popular song about being lifted up on eagle's wings comes from, it's also a reminder that waiting can be spiritually renewing rather than doctor's-office irritating. Waiting requires intentionality and discipline and perseverance, which is precisely the role Advent plays in its dual focus of preparation for Christmas and looking forward to the Second Coming of Christ.

I find the ever-popular Advent calendar helpful here. I love Advent calendars because they're simultaneously a great tradition and a wonderful way to mark down the shopping days until Christmas—I mean, the days until we celebrate the birth of our Savior. Of course it took a couple of years watching our boys fight over whose turn it was to open the next window before we realized each one should have his own Advent calendar. Duh.

I remember one year in particular when Zack's Advent calendar became Bryna's to-do list. I'm not quite sure how this happened, but every time he opened a window, he announced we were obligated to do whatever appeared. So on December 5, we had to hang our stockings. Three days later, we had to buy our tree, which, thanks be to God, coincided with the parish Christmas tree sale. One morning, after opening the appropriate window, Zack declared that we must "have mint." Whatever that meant. If he tries this again, there better be snow on the ground when he gets to the snowman window, otherwise we're in trouble.

During Advent we hear so many voices, often including our own, screaming, "I can't wait!" Well, actually we can and we must. Holy waiting is a discipline worth practicing. It can be practiced through increased diligence to prayer and meditation and during periods of silence. Does this seem impossible during this "most wonderful time of the year?" It's not. It means listening more resolutely to the still, small voice within—and ignoring the loud, large voice from beyond that's yelling, "I can't wait!"

Nesting

I f you've ever lived with a pregnant woman, you're familiar with the nesting phenomenon. Expectant mothers can go slightly overboard preparing their homes for the arrival of a new baby. It starts with intense cleaning—and not just your average sweep-the-kitchen-floor and wipe-down-counters cleaning. It's pull-out-the-couch and vacuum-the-ceiling, which then progresses to obsessive organizing.

When Bryna was eight months pregnant with Zack, I remember walking through the hallway in our Baltimore row house looking for her. Instead, I encountered an empty linen closet. She was on the floor with every sheet, towel, comforter, and pillowcase we owned. Closet shelves were being sterilized and lots of sorting was involved. I forgot whatever I thought was so important and went back in the bedroom to hide.

I'm not sure if Mary did any nesting such as tidying up the stable or sweeping up hay. Scripture doesn't mention there being a whole lot of time between arriving in Bethlehem and giving birth to Jesus, but nesting is really a form of preparation, and preparation is hard work.

Advent preparation involves a blend of anticipation, excitement, and anxiety. It sets us slightly on edge, gets our adrenaline pumping, heightens awareness, and keeps us alert. Of course, Advent isn't just about getting ready for a single big day; it's also a reminder to be vigilant in leading a life of anticipatory preparation and joy.

Like most families, our preparations for Christmas aren't just spiritual; they come in a box. Or more precisely, a bunch of boxes up in the attic. I find this section of our storage closet spookier than the single box of Halloween decorations. The boxes seem to multiply each year, and I swear we have enough ornaments to trim every tree on our block.

Bryna is, thankfully, the steward of these boxes. She knows what's in them, and, while I'm happy to haul them downstairs, I do my best to stay out of the way when they get unpacked. I recognize some of what's inside—like the icicle lights I wrestle with each year and the papier-mache golden reindeer that's missing part of an antler—but much of it I swear I've

never seen before. What happens next is a kind of
spiritual nesting. The decorations are carefully placed
on tabletops and in windows, and the stockings are
hung by the chimney with care in hopes that baby
Jesus soon will be there.

A balance is needed between practical and spiritual preparation. It's one thing to pray a lot and go to church every Sunday in Advent. You won't ever hear this parish priest complaining about too much of that. But the decorations are important since they communicate that something unusual and exciting is about to take place. Both children and adults respond to the tangible preparations of December. When the tree goes up and the lights go on, that old Christmas magic comes alive—but if we become focused solely on the tinsel and the placement of the mistletoe, then the connection to our Savior's birth is lost. Together, however, practical and spiritual preparations bring even more joy to the season by heightening the anticipation.

At church, this involves putting up greenery during Advent. We gather a group together for what I always refer to as the "Greening of the Church." Wreaths adorn the walls, garlands are strung, and trees are set up. This process used to be called the "Hanging of the Greens" until a new family named "Green" started attending.

Sometimes the boys will help out at church, but they're much more interested in tree trimming at home—at least when it's on their terms. Ben and

Zack both have their favorite ornaments that have become part of the trimming ritual. Every year, Ben reverently places the Baltimore Ravens football-shaped ornament onto a visible branch, while Zack seeks out the one of Snoopy playing a saxophone. They help out with the lower branches until I go to change the Christmas music in the other room, at which point they flee to video game heaven. I like to hang the ornament we bought for Ben while on vacation in Wisconsin before he was born. It reminds of my first encounter with a nesting mother-to-be, and it sends a brief chill down my spine.

O Christmas Tree

When I lived in New York, my parish held an annual Christmas tree sale on the first two weekends of December. I always spent some time working at it because a) it was a lot of fun; and b) I got to wield a chain saw. Parish ministry affords few opportunities to lose a limb; offering "fresh cut" trees is about the only physical danger in church work. So of course I would stare the danger down with steely eyes while Bryna rolled hers.

My only real shortcoming at the tree sale was tying trees onto people's cars. I must have missed knot tying during my short-lived stint as a Cub Scout, so either someone else would deal with the twine or the customer risked losing the tree as they pulled out of the church parking lot. This actually happened to parishioners one year—their tree ended up on Route 9.

The parish did get fabulous trees: they came from the same small tree farm in Pennsylvania every year, and we always sold out. Sure, it helped that we undercut the Methodists, but our trees and wreaths were also much fresher. I know, because we sent spies.

While most people were incredibly gracious and families were filled with joy as they chose their tree, there were always several exceptions. Invariably a few people came looking for "the perfect tree." They were incredibly insistent about this, as if their entire Christmas depended upon arboreal perfection. Of course no tree was ever good enough. They'd spend an hour looking through every single tree on the lot, treating the church volunteers like the hired help at some high-end boutique on Rodeo Drive. "No, that one's not right. Show me that one. Turn it around. This one's too full; that one's not full enough. Don't you have anything that smells better?" And there was nothing we could do but grit our teeth and keep a smile plastered on our face as they tested the limits of Christian charity.

Sometimes they would leave with a tree; sometimes they'd go away disappointed. I was always saddened when I encountered this because these folks were truly seeking something, trying to fill a void in their lives that can only be satisfied by a relationship with Jesus Christ. The irony was that they were standing twenty-five feet from a church a few weeks before Christmas, and yet they completely missed the point of the entire season. The reality is that they won't ever have the picture-perfect Christmas as long as they try to achieve it through external, human means, like the perfect tree, the perfect gift, or the perfect dinner.

AND HOW DO I GET INSIDE MY CAR?

The other advantage of holding a tree sale was that I determined a new measure for the ultimate act of faith. The trees all came bundled up, so we would open enough to display and stack the others off to the side. I once suggested to Bryna that we simply take a bundled one, sight unseen, from the pile and throw it onto the roof of our car. What an act of trust! What an act of faith! She wasn't interested.

Jesus is most often met in the very messiness of Christmas. We sanitize and sentimentalize it, perhaps, with our miniature nativity sets neatly arranged on the mantelpiece while ignoring the muck and messiness of the stable. But it is to the brokenness and imperfection of our lives that God entered the world in human form. That's the Christmas miracle. If God wanted the "perfect" Christmas, Jesus would have been born in a palace, not a stable, and he would have been born to a princess, not to an unwed teenage mother. But Christmas is about genuine relationship with the divine rather than superficial perfection. If that's your goal, you're better off buying a perfectly shaped fake tree at Target.

These are the things I would reflect upon as I lugged another eight-foot tree toward the waiting roof of a Chevy Suburban. I'd snap out of it as soon as the

IT'S JUST PERFECT.

next car pulled into the lot and an expectant family poured out of their mini-van.

The boys also had a great time working at the tree sale. Okay, I use the term "working" loosely, but they did have fun. They'd run around the trees, soaking in the tree-selling atmosphere, throwing snowballs at each other and at me, drinking hot chocolate, throwing sticks onto the open fire, and asking me incessantly whether they could use the chain saw. Not this year, guys.

Their favorite thing was to be run through the baler. There's just something about seeing your kids laugh hysterically while wrapped up in plastic Christmas tree netting. Of course there are days when I think having a baler for home use might not be such a bad idea.

Miracle on 34th Street

Four blocks from our former home in Baltimore is a pedestrian stretch of red brick row houses. During most of the year, it is largely ignored. There's nothing remarkable about a block of row houses in Charm City; Baltimore is full of similar streets with their trademark marble steps. But this is 34th Street and so, inspired by the movie, this little block of brick row houses lives up to its name in a dramatic way every December.

I'm not sure how or when it started, but by the first week in December the whole street is decked out with lights and Christmas displays. Believe me, it's nothing understated—simplicity and subtlety are not the goals. This display is something altogether different, perhaps even miraculous. It has become such an institution in Baltimore that the electric utility company, in a rare display of Christmas spirit, waives their fee for the month—which is a good thing because after gazing in wide-wondered awe, your first question would be, "How do they pay their electric bill?"

This display is extraordinary. Not tasteful, mind you, but extraordinary. Imagine the gaudiest display of Christmas lights, ornaments, and statues you've ever seen, then magnify it by about ten and you're coming close to Christmas on 34th Street. Blinking colored lights, strung from house-to-house, form a canopy across the street; there are several eight-

foot-tall plastic figures of everyone from Frosty the Snowman to Santa to Rudolph. There's usually a Christmas Elvis somewhere, and one family puts out an impressive display of decorated hubcaps each year. It's quite a sight.

And forget about trying to get through the neighborhood on the last few days before Christmas; traffic piles up, cars inch slowly past as holiday gawkers stare out the windows, people on foot stream up and down the street, and the place is a magnet for television reporters sending live updates back to the anchor desk. Our boys were completely mesmerized by the display—with a light snow falling, it may have been the North Pole. If Santa's workshop was in Vegas.

Something that's easy to forget amid the impressive wattage of any over-the-top Christmas display or even the simplest white candle in the window of a Victorian home is what light has to do with Christmas in the first place. Every single bulb points in some small way to the light of Christ. I try to remind the boys of this on those nights we drive around town looking for the tackiest displays, which is something of a hobby of ours. I tell them that each light points to Jesus, just as John writes, "the light shines in the darkness" (John 1:5).

John is, of course, talking about a different kind of light, one that not only shines through darkness but also through power outages; it's a light that can never be turned off with a switch or become unplugged: the Light of Christ.

I had a seminary professor who couldn't stand the song, "This Little Light of Mine." It wasn't because it's the Christian equivalent of "It's a Small World After All." He rejected it on theological grounds, proclaiming, "The light is neither little, nor yours." And, of course, he has a point: one of the foundational images of the Christian faith is regarding Christ as the light of the world who shatters the darkness of sin. Unlike the strands of Christmas lights that get hauled out every year, this light cannot be contained. It burns brighter than any Christmas display, no matter the time, effort, and voltage that goes into it. Yet this light is not merely metaphorical; it's something we can all experience. It burns within us and can be as accessible as flipping a light switch.

I'm sure I'll always think about 34th Street in Baltimore at Christmas time. As outrageous as it is, there is also something magical about it, perhaps because a group of neighbors join together to create such a spectacle. And while it may not be how I'd like to spend my time before Christmas, a tremendous amount of spirit and energy goes into setting the whole thing up. You won't see an illuminated Christmas Elvis on the front lawn of our home next year. My personal taste in Christmas decor, Bryna's reaction, and my ineptitude with things electrical preclude that. But maybe we'll try to put some Christmas lights on the exterior of the house next Christmas. I don't have a problem with it, as long as it points to, in some small way, the true light of the world that is Jesus Christ.

Say Cheese!

A couple years ago our attempt to take a Christmas card picture was a total disaster. We tried for one of those perfect cards. We endured the boys' arguments over putting on button-down shirts and dress pants and the whining over combing hair. We moved the couch, brushed our dog Delilah, and put on her Christmas collar. We cajoled, threatened, and bribed—with dog treats and video game privileges.

Still, it was horrible. If one of the boys wasn't making an "I hate this" face, the other was mugging for the camera like an over-stimulated monkey. And on the exceedingly rare occasion that they both looked, if not happy, then at least not like they'd just sucked on a lemon, Delilah ruined the shot by licking herself.

This experience was a good reminder that perfection is overrated. We usually send out semi-candid shots that try to capture the boys in their natural habitat rather than unnaturally posed photographs. Not that they'd consent to sitting still while some cheesy

photographer implored them to say "cheese." I can't imagine them sitting happily together on a fake sled wearing matching sweaters and holding giant candy canes.

I admit I like receiving Christmas cards. They're a great way to connect with people you hear from only once a year, and I always love sorting through the ones at my mother's house to check up on long-lost family friends. In many ways, Facebook has rendered this practice obsolete. You used to be a long-lost friend

I heard from only once a year, but now, in addition to the annual Christmas card, I know precisely when you last went to the dentist.

There's always been something superficial, however, about the whole Christmas card charade. The accompanying letter shares only the good news. So you hear about the son who got into Harvard and the daughter who won a ballet competition and the fabulous family vacation to Maui, but you don't get anything about marital strife or job loss or a child's bout with depression. Just once, I'd like to receive a Christmas card that would admit to the brokenness and need for healing along with the celebrations of life. If, instead of "Say cheese!" the photographer said "Show us how you really feel!" I guarantee fewer cheesy grins would pass through mail slots.

We haven't sent out a Christmas letter in years. Not because we didn't want to brag about Ben's ability to read *Anna Karenina* in Russian when he was two, or Zack's becoming a kindergarten grandmaster chess player, but because we're too busy and too tired to get it together in time.

Maybe some year we'll send out one of our ill-fated Christmas card attempts which, if nothing else, would certainly be more authentic. It's okay to let the chaos and brokenness shine through every once in awhile, even around the holidays. Two days after our disastrous photo shoot, Aunt Liz took a great snapshot of the boys wearing football helmets, a close-up of their faces inside the masks. Bryna and I looked at each other, said "That's it!" and ordered the cards. Not very Christmas-y but definitely more representative of that particular stage of life.

Reflection & Discussion

1 While impatience is particularly acute in children, we're all impatient. What are you most impatient about and how do you deal with it? Does your own impatience distract you from living in the present? If so, how?

2 What are some of your cherished family rituals around Christmas? Is there an adequate balance between your practical and spiritual preparations? In what ways could you even out the balance?

3 Do you have any vivid memories of Christmas trees past? Do you sometimes find yourself spending more time on creating the perfect Christmas than on nurturing your relationship with God and others? Describe a favorite tree-trimming memory from your childhood. How are things different for you today?

4 Do you hang Christmas decorations outside of your home? Why or why not? What kind of decorations? Have you ever made the connection between Christmas lights and the Light of Christ? How could you view hanging outdoor lights as a spiritual act?

5 Do you send out Christmas cards each year? What about an annual letter? Why or why not? What image do you think you project to others? What might be closer to the reality? What will your Christmas card look like this year?

II. CAST OF CHARACTERS

Dog in the Manger

There's a great scene in the movie *Diner* in which Kevin Bacon's character gets drunk and punches out the Three Wise Men. In his underwear. It all takes place at a life-sized nativity scene outside a church in a respectable Baltimore neighborhood.

Now I'm not encouraging you to go out and do likewise, but there is something about this scene that warms the heart, and I'm not just referring to the Christmas spirits involved. If nothing else, Kevin Bacon's character, Fenwick, is *engaged* with the nativity scene. He is literally in the midst of it, especially when he lies down in the manger. And while our engagement is hopefully a bit more metaphorical, so often we fail to engage in a real and meaningful way. Instead we set up our little crèches and admire them from afar. They may well be beautifully crafted, but when we put them on the mantle and tell our kids to look but not touch, we miss the power of the Christmas story, a power unleashed only when

we engage it. Not by punching out the Magi, but by incorporating the message of salvation into our lives, by meeting Jesus as he first comes to us as a child but ultimately as the risen Christ. Otherwise a nativity scene is merely a bunch of statues, be they miniature works of art or giant pieces of plastic.

Public nativity scenes have become the subjects of lawsuits in towns across America, and that's too bad because insisting crèches be put up in public places strips them of their power. They become reduced to political footballs that do nothing to honor the miracle of Christmas. When I lived in New York, our town of seven thousand became embroiled in the requisite "culture wars" debate about public holiday displays, complete with an article about the controversy in *The*

New York Times. Some guy wanted to donate a large crèche scene, the village trustees turned him down, and in the true spirit of Christmas, he sued them. We ended up with a "non-religious holiday display" consisting of a large decorated tree with a star on top alongside a huge metallic dreidel. How inspiring.

The other danger of the crèche is that it neglects the scandal of the nativity. What took place in Bethlehem over two thousand years ago was more than just a quaint Christmas card scene of a newborn child and his family. It was God entering the world as a helpless infant born in a manger. God didn't come to us through the worldly splendor of a palace; rather God slipped into the midst of humanity in a small and insignificant town far from the seat of power.

Some reality testing is helpful here: stables are not precious places; they are dirty and smelly. "Manger" is euphemism for feeding trough; the phrase "cattle lowing" is just a poetic way to say cows are mooing, and as every parent knows, with a newborn there's no such thing as a "silent night." But none of this takes away from the miracle, and, if anything, it is that much more poignant because Christ entered our world, not *Fantasy Island.* He entered a place with real people and real passions, not a world where the Three Wise Men kneel in handcrafted glory. It's a reminder that engaging our faith can be messy, which is again why I like that scene from *Diner*. Jesus is with us—not just when we act respectably, not just when we gaze from afar, but in moments of anger and grief and pain and joy and celebration.

Every year, Bryna and Ben fight over baby Jesus. Bryna believes that Jesus shouldn't be placed in the crèche until Christmas Eve, so we have the scene all set up in the living room, but Jesus is on the bookshelf. Unless Ben wanders into the living room. Then baby Jesus is placed back into the manger since Ben likes the whole scene to be set up properly. So for a couple of weeks, Jesus is the object of this good-natured tug-of-war. I stay above the fray by avoiding the whole conversation.

But actually, they're both right. I prefer to keep the baby Jesus out of the crèche until Christmas just to emphasize the void that gets filled with Jesus' arrival. Of course I also don't like the Three Wise Men getting to the crèche before Epiphany on January 6, so you can call me a nativity scene fundamentalist. But Ben's theory is true as well, since even as we await the arrival of the Christ Child, Jesus is fully present with us.

Beyond the usual suspects, we've had a variety of crèche crashers over the years. One year it was overrun with superheroes; another it was the whole cast of Star Wars; and most years Delilah sticks her nose into things, literally becoming a "dog in the manger." It looks a bit odd when people come over and expect the perfect clergy family décor, but I never remove the action figures. I like to see the boys engaging the story of the nativity even if their version is slightly apocryphal. Did Luke Skywalker really show up in his X-wing fighter to whisk Melchior back home? Perhaps not. But while there might not have been any room at the inn on that first Christmas Eve, there's always plenty of space available around the manger. Even if you live in a parallel universe.

Crying Out

What would you do if John the Baptist showed up at Christmas dinner? You couldn't help but notice, right? A large man wearing nothing but camel hair would tend to stick out.

There's nothing particularly discreet about this forerunner of the Messiah. He's not known as John the Episcopalian after all, and crying out in the wilderness day after day can get in the way of tending to personal hygiene. So when this hulk of a man with locusts and wild honey matted into his beard sits down next to you, how do you respond? Call the cops? Pass the yams?

John the Baptist plays an important role during Advent. He reminds us that preparing to receive Christ into the world is not always a neat and tidy business; it can be messy and disorderly. He reminds us of the urgency and stirs us out of complacency. We sometimes need a larger (and louder) than life figure to keep us focused on what really matters. (Hint: this transcends the question of whether or not to spike the egg nog).

The first parish I served was a big church in the heart of Baltimore, across from which a street preacher would often set up shop and read passages of scripture in a booming voice. I never did have a conversation with him. My initial impression was that he was a little bit "off," but there were days when I wondered which of us had the more effective ministry.

He was bringing the Word of God directly to the world. Street Preacher boldly stood out on the corner, proclaiming scripture to anyone who'd listen, much like John the Baptist who preached baptism for the repentance of sins to anyone passing by. I, on the other hand, was decked out in expensive vestments handcrafted

in England and spoke only to those venturing into a large, Italian Romanesque building on Charles Street.

I'm not saying this man was a prophet. I don't know what he was or how he viewed his ministry.

But, as John the Baptist reminds us, the truth can be revealed in surprising ways—sometimes through a loud preacher on the banks of the River Jordan and sometimes in a humble manger in the middle of Bethlehem.

John the Baptist is loud, even louder than Uncle Eddie at Christmas dinner, because he needs to be. To speak truth to a skeptical, distracted audience takes both courage and volume. Human beings are a distracted lot, so you can see what drove John the Baptist to shout above the din to proclaim the advent of something new.

We are not always the best listeners; there are competing interests and demands for our attention. There are many messages out there, especially in December: sales, Christmas parties, school holiday shows, family demands. We need someone willing to rise above the din and bring us back to the basics of our faith. Otherwise the kernel of truth gets lost amid the cacophony.

Ben and Zack often wonder why we don't erect giant inflatable lawn ornaments during December like some of their friends' families. Well, I just don't like them, and I much prefer them in a state of deflation so it looks like some sort of Christmas massacre where Frosty the Snowman, Yuletide Shrek, and Rudolph have gone down in a hail of BB's. But I have always thought it would be great to sneak an inflatable John the Baptist onto one of these lawns right alongside eight-foot tall Frosty. The contrast between the one crying out in the wilderness proclaiming the arrival of the Messiah and the one whose presence announces the arrival of the Christmas-industrial complex is too poetic to ignore.

Kids learn from an early age that screaming above the crowd is an effective way to attract attention. The squeaky wheel gets the chicken nugget. I don't believe John the Baptist would be crying out for fried, processed chicken if he sat down at your table, but bringing us back to the basics of our faith is worth making a scene over.

Something about Mary

There's something about Mary. It goes beyond the statues, the oil paintings, and the icons—some beautiful, some paragons of kitsch. How the mother of Jesus ends up as a plastic statue on the dashboard of a Chevy Impala or seen in a grilled cheese sandwich in an Idaho diner is one of life's great mysteries, but it does speak to Mary's power and allure.

At first glance, she's an odd choice to bear God's son. You'd think God might have chosen someone with better credentials—someone with royal blood or political power or maybe someone with gobs of cash. The mother of Jesus has none of these. She's poor, she's pregnant, she's a woman, she's a teenager, and she will soon become an unwed mother. In the eyes of society, she doesn't count, yet in the eyes of God she is the chosen vehicle of salvation.

Maybe there's something about mothers in general. There's a reason every psychiatrist wants to plumb the depths of the relationship with our mothers; it's a bond that informs how we live out our lives in ways we can barely even grasp. Of course, as a father, I want to scream at every therapist I meet, "What about a dad's relationship with the kids? We can screw them up too!" Perhaps mothers have a unique relationship with Mary at Christmas—they can relate to Mary's experience of motherhood and they know better than anyone that while it may have been a holy night, that first Christmas Eve was certainly not silent. Giving birth rarely is, especially without the epidural.

At our house, mom plays a vital role at Christmas. Since dad works on Christmas Eve and Christmas morning, Bryna is as exhausted as I am by late afternoon on Christmas Day. Her responsibilities are slightly different from mine but no less critical. I work to bring the spirit of God to people through liturgy and preaching; Bryna works to make the family Christmas celebration memorable. Part of our Yuletide celebration is the traditional late afternoon fight over who gets to take the first nap.

Like all mothers, it's impossible to ignore Mary at Christmastime, because when it comes to the nativity story, Mary's a player. It's hard to imagine anyone else being more in the mix. Her cries pierce the Bethlehem night, bringing the savior into the world. But, as mothers

know, this birth was nine or ten months in the making. For Mary, it begins earlier, when the angel Gabriel shares the stunning news that she will bear God's son.

She basically asks "why me?" as she greets Gabriel's message with fear, confusion, questioning, and finally

acceptance. There's a reason Mary is revered for her humility, thoughtfulness, and discipleship—she is so fully human in this encounter with Gabriel. There is something so authentic in her uncertainty and hesitation. The range of emotions flashes through her, and she needs the angel's assurance to not be afraid. Her first response isn't acquiescence; it's to take a step back and ponder. Hers is a thoughtful and discerning faith, not a hasty or blind one, and ultimately God uses this girl to make a bold point: for God, nothing is impossible.

Mary's model is a helpful one for us as we meet God through the people and events of our daily lives. It's okay to be fearful, to take time to ponder what is being asked of us, to live into the pregnant pauses that mark our lives of faith. But also in the end, we are asked to trust in God and say, along with Mary, "Here am I, the servant of the Lord; let it be with me according to your word" (Luke 1:38). I'm not sure why this inspires the kitsch of a glow-in-the-dark nightlight, but there's just something about Mary.

Holy Bystander

J oseph doesn't get much press. He's the forgotten one in the Christmas story, and the only time people think about him is when the family crèche is unpacked. He's easy to overlook since he's the one at the bottom of the box. The placement usually goes: Mary, baby Jesus, the three kings, the angel, a shepherd or two, some sheep, and, oh, right, Joseph. Then we move a couple of sheep over and place him awkwardly next to Mary, as if he's an unwelcome guest intruding on the holy vibe. People brought gifts to Jesus, they had kind words for Mary, but they probably didn't know what to say to Joseph. They certainly couldn't say, "I think he has your eyes," because, of course, the baby didn't—Joseph wasn't the father.

Joseph is like a holy bystander, which I think sounds better than sacred loiterer. But he may well have felt like a bystander to the whole scene—supportive of Mary, excited and nervous at the prospect of raising this child but really not too clear on his role in the whole affair.

So Joseph often gets lost in the Christmas shuffle. He's like the Mrs. Claus of Christmas—nice to have around but not really necessary. In fact, at our church a few years ago, we nearly didn't have Joseph in the Christmas pageant. For some reason most of our pageant-aged kids were girls, or at least they were the ones who agreed to participate. As it was, we had to go with the Angel Gabrielle. I was lamenting this at the dinner table a few weeks before Christmas when Ben stunned me by saying, "I'll be Joseph." Wow. This is the same kid who was all set to be a king one year and then backed out at the very last minute, so Jesus didn't get any myrrh.

But Joseph does have a critical role in this story. He serves as a model of how to hear and respond to the word of God. And sometimes just standing around is a worthy spiritual discipline. It means we're present and attentive and ready to be called upon, which isn't a bad posture for any of us in our relationship with God. In Joseph's case, it allows him to be used by God in a very unique way and for a very specific purpose. In the Gospel of Matthew, an angel of the Lord appears to Joseph in a dream, shares the unbelievable news that Mary has conceived a child by the Holy Spirit, and proclaims that the son she bears is to be named Jesus. Talk about waking up with a start. But Joseph is faithful to God's desire, and the boy is named Jesus rather than Joseph of Nazareth Jr.

Naming someone or something is a big deal—kids love naming everything, from stuffed animals to pet ferrets. Naming a child is a huge responsibility for parents since, for one thing, it's permanent, and for

another, it subtly informs the identity of the child. Bryna and I spent a long time debating names both times she was pregnant.

As a kid, I remember being fascinated with the other names my parents considered. To think I could have gone through life with an entirely different identity. I'm thrilled they came to their senses and didn't go with their second choice: Dylan. For Dylan Thomas, not Bob Dylan, in case you were wondering.

I'm not sure how much of this Ben picked up when he played Joseph that year. But any kid who gets coerced into being Joseph can certainly relate to what it's like to be a holy bystander. And that's not a bad thing.

Reflection & Discussion

1 Do you set up a crèche during Advent? What are your family traditions surrounding it? Which character do you most identify with in the nativity scene? Why?

2 What are the competing demands and messages you must deal with in the weeks leading up to Christmas? How do you attend to your faith life at this time of year? Are there measures you could take to give the spiritual message a higher priority?

3 What role does Mary play in your spiritual life? Do you reflect about her outside the seasons of Advent and Christmas? What lessons can you learn from her story that could be of use in your own life?

4 Have you ever thought much about Joseph's role in the Christmas story? What parts of his character do you most identify with? What does being a holy bystander mean to you?

III. CHRISTMAS EVE AND BEYOND

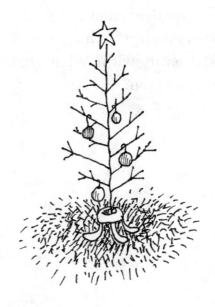

How the Grinch Kept Christmas

When he was four-and-a-half, Ben was addicted to the Grinch. Through some rehab (i.e., getting older), he's made peace with his compulsion and is now in a much better place. His addiction started out innocently enough when a December trip to the local library yielded a VHS tape of the 1966 television version of the Dr. Seuss classic. For one solid week, the length of time before it was due back, Ben practically lived in Whoville. He insisted on watching the Grinch movie nearly every waking moment, though Bryna and I Grinchishly limited his viewing pleasure to twice a day.

In between screenings, Ben pranced around the house playing Grinch. This involved taking a cloth sack and stuffing it with ornaments, stockings, and assorted Christmas decorations in a concerted effort to "steal Christmas." While I sat in a living room chair observing the proceedings, Ben would gleefully dump the contents on my lap. I, of course, was the Grinch's overloaded sleigh. He would then climb on top of me and hitch up his dog Max by dangling an unused strand of Christmas tree lights onto the floor.

Then the dreaded video return date came. Amid much protestation, we slid the video into the library drop box. But I had a plan. I nearly tore the house apart, but I found my old childhood copy of *How the Grinch Stole Christmas*. The book cover was faded, and I had written my first name on the inside cover in what was clearly a struggle and triumph of early penmanship. We entered a new phase of Grinch obsession, and every night for weeks, long after the end of the Christmas season, the Grinch was part of our bedtime ritual. By the time the Grinch was mercifully returned to the attic, Ben and I were reciting large sections of it to one another over breakfast.

When you read something over and over again, you start to see things that may or may not exist, and the more I read the story, the more I started viewing the Grinch in spiritual terms. Pitchers and catchers had reported for spring training, and I was still reading about all the Whos down in Whoville. In the midst of this daze, I started to think there is more to the Grinch's story than a dig on rampant consumerism.

The Grinch, after all, is ultimately a story of conversion. The Grinch has a conversion experience atop Mount Crumpit that is both powerful and swift. Standing in the snow, his puzzler sore from puzzling, the Grinch literally and metaphorically has a change of heart. The proverbial scales drop from his eyes, and he sees something he never saw before: Christmas really doesn't just come from a store. His heart not only grows three sizes, but the Grinch also is indelibly and irrevocably transformed by this mountaintop experience.

This Seussian story is also one of forgiveness. The moment the Grinch repents his Grinchlike ways, the Whos unconditionally welcome him into their community. This is, for the Grinch, a moment of grace. He has sinned in his foolish attempt to steal Christmas because he has tried to take something away that was not in his power to take. Rather than trying to play God, as human sinners do, he tries to play Santa Claus. But the Whos believe in something more profound than presents and trimmings and trappings.

The idea of the Grinch sharing a meal with the Whos is as improbable as tax collectors and sinners sharing a meal with the Messiah, yet this is exactly what happens in scripture and in the story of the Grinch. After conversion, repentance, and forgiveness, the Grinch takes his place at the table as an honored guest. His past offenses have been wiped away, and he enters into a new life. As a full participant in the feast, he breaks bread with the Whos, a symbol of his full inclusion in the community, and he is invited to share in the sacramental meal of the Whos' Christmas roast beast.

On the last page of the book, we see the converted Grinch at the seat of honor, carving the roast beast. There's a Who seated at his left hand and one at his

right and framed above is a large wreath—first seen on page one—that hovers over his head like a halo. The transformation is complete.

It is possible I've gotten a bit carried away here. I can only plead an inordinate amount of time spent with the Grinch, but I encourage you to experience this wonderful tale anew this Christmas. Just know that once you open this book, you may be reading it well into the spring.

Holy Hangover

S o what does a clergy family do on Christmas Eve? Well, our tradition is to pull out the crystal and silver and order Chinese food. It works for everyone: Bryna doesn't have to cook, I get fed in between the three services, the table looks festive, and the kids pig out on sesame beef. Alright, the kids don't actually eat Chinese, so we end up making Christmas Eve chicken nuggets, and they gorge themselves on fortune cookies and those Chinese noodles that come with the wonton soup. After the 4:00 p.m. pageant service, we come home and wait for the guy from Pacific Palace to show up. Nothing says "Angels we have heard on high" like an order of General Tso's chicken.

The hardest part for me is that Midnight Mass starts way past my bedtime. Whoever began this tradition clearly didn't have kids. So I eat shrimp fried rice, drink coffee, and wait for the kids to go to sleep. Usually they're still pinging off the walls by the time I head back to church for the late service, and I always feel guilty leaving Bryna to handle the boys' adrenaline-based shenanigans. The struggle of dealing with kids at Christmas is hardly news to parents of young children. Watching their unadulterated excitement is joyful; trying to wrestle them to bed on Christmas Eve is not. The anticipation of Santa's impending visit combined with a candy-cane sugar high is a powerful elixir. Add in the holy chaos of a Christmas pageant, and the kids are flying.

Up until very recently, Ben and Zack still looked forward to participating in the pageant. Ours is pretty standard fare—the usual suspects are all there along with myriad sheep, shepherds, and angels. Zack's never been anything but one of the three kings. It's the only role he'll play, which meant we had four kings one year. Ben's a bit more versatile—besides that one year he offered to play Joseph, he's been both a king and a shepherd.

One pageant highlight was the year King Zack did the "Lambeau Leap." He told us he was going to "leap into the stands" like a Packers player following a touchdown in Green Bay and, by God, he did. After the Magi presented their gifts of gold, frankincense, and myrrh, Zack turned around and jumped into

Bryna's arms in the front pew. He then went right back into character, kneeling before the manger.

I always wake up on Christmas morning with a "holy hangover." No alcohol's involved, but after all the services, it feels like I've been clobbered with a giant candy cane, especially when the boys come bounding into our room at 6:00 a.m. Parents of older teenagers tell me they have to literally wake their kids up to open presents on Christmas morning, though at this stage of life I can't even imagine that; it sounds so civilized.

The year of Zack's Lambeau Leap, we told the boys not to bother us until 7:00 a.m; we even put an alarm clock in their room. They could get their stockings before then, but they'd been ordered not to bother us until the magic number came up seven. This edict was utterly disobeyed, but at least they slept in until 6:40 a.m. I could live with that...and did.

My problem was the visit at 3:09 a.m. Are you kidding me? Both boys came into our room in the wee hours, asking if they could go downstairs to see if Santa had come. I nearly had to block the stairwell to prevent their stampede, and my only recourse was the desperate parental reminder that if Santa Claus sees them, they could say *sayonara* to getting any presents.

They reluctantly returned to their bunk beds, and I had to stay there for another thirty minutes while Ben squirmed, and Zack announced the new time on the clock every two minutes, while asking, "Has it been four hours yet?"

The good news about them getting up early is that we can open all the gifts at a leisurely pace (if tearing off gift wrap like a ravenous pack of dogs can be considered leisurely) before I head back to church for the 10:00 am service. Hopefully they'll come to see that Jesus is the ultimate Christmas gift, but for now, I just pray their new toys will keep them occupied long enough for me to get in a late afternoon Christmas nap.

Post-Christmas Blues

I s there anything more depressing than de-trimming a Christmas tree? No one in my family ever wants to do this job. Obviously the boys are nowhere to be seen, and even Delilah the dog makes herself scarce. As yuletide traditionalists, we keep ours up through Epiphany (January 6), even if every single needle has fallen off, at which point it's unceremoniously stripped and hauled down the driveway where it waits for pickup by the town sanitation department. O Christmas Tree, O the indignity.

This year's tree removal was like years past. Bryna notes the date, fights off her own post-Christmas angst, and then goes into uber de-trimming mode. I just stand back, speak when spoken to, and do what I'm told. On her cue, I wrestle the tree out of the stand while it spews needles all over the place (note to self: haul it out top first next year), and I get covered with sap that I can't get off my hands for months (another note to self: use gloves next year). By the time I've

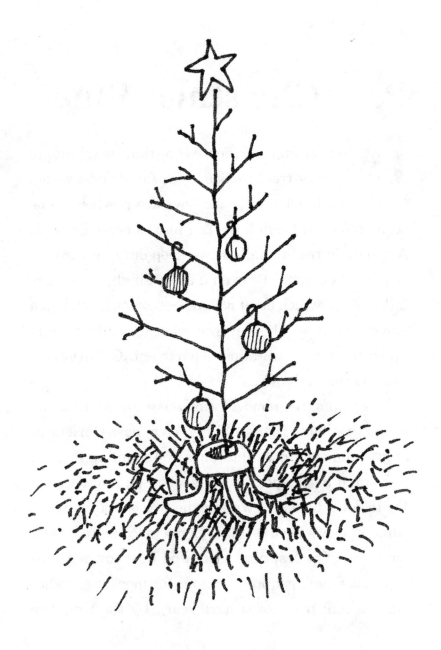

done this, the boxes of ornaments are sitting in front of the attic door, Bryna's not-so-subtle hint.

For all the hype and frenzy of the pre-Christmas build-up, it's amazing how quickly it all comes crashing down. Well, except for the front door wreath. Either people no longer use their front doors or they neglect them, but well into March you'll see browning wreaths adorning doors all around your neighborhood. Call me a stickler, but my general rule is that if it's Lent, take down the Christmas wreath! If it makes it until Easter, you may as well just leave it up until next Christmas.

Go into a store on the days following Christmas, and it's like Christmas never happened. Were all those tinsel-clad angels and dish towel-headed shepherds mere hallucinations?

The trick is holding onto that Christmas spirit year-round. Christ's incarnation, God's coming into the world in human form, isn't relegated to the twelve days of Christmas. If so, what would be the point? If the Christmas spirit doesn't even have the shelf-life of your average fruitcake, something's wrong. Thinking about the real message of Christmas while hauling down exterior icicle lights isn't a bad spiritual exercise. The sales are over, the lights are off, and the kids are back to the normal routine. Threats that they'll get coal in their stockings if they don't behave are no longer effective, and the extended family has gone home. Hopefully.

Kids aren't immune to the post-Christmas blues. Their issues have nothing to do with eating too much Yule log cake or maxing out credit cards. But like any event with a massive build-up, there's going to be a let-down. Ask most kids what they got for Christmas a few weeks after the blessed event, and they can perhaps recall one or two big-ticket items, but the rest fades quickly into the background. They remember the new set of skis, but that book from Aunt Wanda about the Iditarod? Not so much.

Christmas Day at our house isn't complete until one of the kids looks around at the wrapping paper strewn all over the floor and asks incredulously, "Is that it?" And, yes, that is it. Well, at least until we go over to Grandma's for lunch and discover that Santa accidentally dropped a few gifts off at the wrong house. Only then is it really "it." Then the kids tune me out as I explain for the umpteenth time that Christmas is about more than the presents, which they know in theory, or at least until the last gift has been torn open.

I don't think we get the "is that it?" cry because our kids are particularly greedy. Rather, I think opening the last gift leads to a certain emptiness. After all the momentum to Christmas, after all the hype, it's suddenly over. There's a void that we all feel, regardless of age or the number of presents we received. Of course Jesus fills the void, but that's hard to see in the immediate aftermath of balled-up wrapping paper shoved into a garbage bag. And once the last gift is opened, the clock starts ticking on the de-trimming.

My teetering atop a ladder, pulling down colored lights above the front door, has become an annual spectator sport as the boys watch me out the window and laugh. I guess I'm glad to offer them a distraction from the reality that Christmas is officially over. Being sensitive to their post-Christmas funk doesn't make the whining any easier as we count the days until school begins, but it does offer some context and gives us an opportunity to reflect with them on what a great Christmas it's been. They may not recall every single present they received, but any less-than-stellar memories fade quickly and soon enough we'll be back to threatening coal in the stockings for bad behavior.

Star Gazing

Let's face it: they'd make lousy baby gifts. Gold is a choking hazard, a flaming pot of frankincense would cause third-degree burns, and no one even knows what myrrh is. Perhaps on their way to Bethlehem, the Magi should have stopped by Babies-R-Us. At least then they could have found something Mary and Joseph could have actually used, like a new set of swaddling clothes, a Diaper Genie, or a Noah's Ark mobile for the manger.

On January 6 we celebrate the Epiphany, which marks both the arrival of the three kings and serves as the official end to the Christmas season. You remember "The Twelve Days of Christmas" (the song that is the Yuletide equivalent of "Ninty-Nine Bottles of Beer on the Wall")? Well, Epiphany marks the end of the twelve days, even though this fact is often overlooked in our rush to take down the tree and cart it off to the town dump.

The Three Wise Men end up in Christmas Eve pageants throughout the land, even though that's not true to the gospel. Most pageants are a medley of gospel stories—nowhere in the Bible do shepherds and Wise Men show up at the same time together. Making that change in the Christmas Eve pageant would be a losing battle—and who wants to fight with the director and tell parents that there won't be any Wise Men this year? Not me.

And anyway, I think it's fine since our traditional pageants provide a more complete picture of the Christmas story. Still, it's nice to remember that the actual arrival of the Magi occurred twelve days later.

One reason I'm a big fan of Epiphany is the notion of following the Star of Bethlehem. If you've ever tried to follow a star for guidance in a boat or in the woods, and I've done neither, you know the posture involved. You have to look up! Navel gazing or staring at your feet does no good when trying to follow a star, and while this is obvious, how often do we find ourselves metaphorically walking around with our heads down? It's so easy to get caught up in our own needs, our own lives, and our own desires that we fail to look up and out at the broader world.

A myopic view of the world is ultimately a spiritual danger. Looking up draws us into an attitude of awe and wonder; it helps change our perspective, and it, quite literally, allows us to see the world in a new light. For people of faith, this posture keeps us mindful of both the needs of others and our need for the divine presence in our lives, a perspective that sustains and blesses rather than diminishes and narrows.

This is how the Wise Men viewed the world. They were seekers of contact with a force beyond themselves, one they couldn't necessarily understand but which drew them into direct contact with God. We, too, can journey with them during this season of cold and dark because God supplies the light. In the words of the prophet Isaiah, "Arise, shine, for your light has come and the glory of the Lord has dawned upon you" (60:1). When you follow the proverbial Star of Bethlehem, your light has indeed come, and it dawns upon you even in the midst of the coldest New England winter.

Most children are fascinated with telescopes. They like to look up at the sky at night and see the vast universe into which we were placed. Whenever we'd find ourselves out in the country on a clear night, my father would point out the constellations. Those were special moments, although I've since forgotten all their names and can't teach them to my own kids. But taking a child outside on a clear night presents the perfect opportunity to wonder what the Magi might have seen up in the sky and what their journey entailed. A bright star is full of imagination and hope and the wonder and mystery of creation.

Of course the Magi didn't show up in Bethlehem empty-handed. Those strange baby gifts were metaphorical rather than practical. Gold is a symbol of Christ the King; frankincense, an ancient symbol of prayer, highlights the importance of Jesus' relationship with God his Father; and myrrh was an embalming oil used to foreshadow Jesus' death. Sure, a sippy cup and baby monitor would have been more useful. But in light of that bright star, gold, frankincense, and myrrh were the perfect gifts.

Reflection & Discussion

1 What lessons do you see in the classic tale of the Grinch? Do you agree or disagree with any of the points raised? What role does consumerism play in your own Christmas celebration?

2 In what ways do you connect with and/or identify with the Magi? Do you feel a yearning for something beyond the visible? If so, how do you seek it out? In what ways do you see your life as a journey of search and discovery?

CHRISTMAS EVE AND BEYOND 77

3 What does Christmas Eve look like in your home? Are there traditions you would like to incorporate? What do you find the most rewarding/challenging about the night before Christmas?

4 Do you experience a post-Christmas letdown? What strategies do you employ to cope with the void? How does this feeling impact your spiritual life? Who de-trims the tree? When?

Afterword

When I was growing up, every Christmas dinner at our house always included an unexpected guest. My mother insisted on inviting at least one person who had nowhere else to go. Sometimes it was someone we knew—like an elderly friend of my parents who talked too much. At others it was a perfect stranger, at least to me and my brother, like some lonely soul my mother befriended who had just moved to town and didn't have any nearby family. Looking back, this was a kind gesture of Christian hospitality, a way of living out that wonderful line from the letter to the Hebrews: "Do not neglect to show hospitality to strangers, for by doing so some have entertained angels unawares." But it drove me nuts.

While my mother was intent on "entertaining angels unawares," all I wanted was to be enveloped in the family cocoon. I didn't want some stranger piercing the bubble of comfort food, relaxed conversation, and contentedly watching football with a full belly. And I mean that both metaphorically—so that I could just relax and be myself—and physically. It's harder to get away with slouching when a stranger is sitting across from you at the dinner table. Frankly, it felt like a home invasion or at least like having a traditional Christmas card picture taken with mom, dad, the two boys, the dog, and some guy named Ed.

During the Passover Seder meal, Jews always leave an empty seat at the table. The tradition is that it's left for the prophet Elijah in case he happens to wander in and demand some matzo ball soup. Actually it has to do with the belief that Elijah will precede the arrival of the Messiah.

Nonetheless, I've always thought there was something wonderful about leaving a physical place open for the divine presence. When we invite God into our lives in the midst of Christmas chaos, life becomes so much more fulfilling, and the season takes on the meaning that it so richly deserves. Connections are made between the sacred and the secular, between the visible and the invisible, and we recognize there is no situation that excludes space for God.

I hope this brief collection of essays helped bring an extra shot of spirituality to your Christmas season, made you smile, and helped keep the seasonal

madness in perspective. I've found over the years that whatever we do or fail to do in the weeks leading up to Christmas—Santa isn't the only one with a massive to-do list—Jesus always arrives in that manger right on schedule. May God bless you and your loved ones and may you be drawn ever deeper into relationship with Jesus Christ.

About the Author

The Rev. Tim Schenck is rector of the Episcopal Parish of St. John the Evangelist in Hingham, Massachusetts, and the creator of the wildly popular online devotion Lent Madness. A priest since 2000, he writes a syndicated monthly column titled "In Good Faith," blogs regularly at Clergy Family Confidential, and is active on social media where you can follow him on Twitter @FatherTim. Schenck lives in the St. John's rectory, on the South Shore of Boston, with his wife Bryna, their teenage sons Benedict and Zachary, their dog Delilah, and Mimi the ferret.

About the Illustrator

The Rev. Jay Sidebotham is well-known for his cartoons about church life and his animation work on the television cartoon *Schoolhouse Rock*! He is the director of RenewalWorks, a ministry of Forward Movement. He served for many years as rector of Church of the Holy Spirit in Lake Forest, Illinois, and has served congregations in New York City, Washington, D.C., North Carolina, and Rhode Island.

Christmas card trauma.
Over-the-top decorations.
Post-Christmas blues.

With laugh-out-loud humor anchored by spiritual
truths, author Tim Schenck helps us maintain our
spiritual sanity through the often frenetic chaos of
Advent and Christmas. Illustrated by popular cartoonist
Jay Sidebotham, *Dog in the Manger* also explores the
major characters of the season in new ways, including
John the Baptist, Mary, Joseph—and of course, Jesus.

Thoughtful questions following each section make
Dog in the Manger ideal for personal reflection,
seasonal book groups, or a last-minute Christmas gift.

ISBN 978-0-88028-371-7

**Forward
Movement**
www.forwardmovement.org **2208**

9 780880 283717